THE GREETING OF PEACE
REVEALED TO ST. FRANCIS

GIANMARIA POLIDORO

The Greeting
of Peace revealed
to St. Francis

Translation by
Joseph O'Boyle and Paul Reczec

Edizioni Porziuncola

Translation of the book title:
Il saluto rivelato a Francesco

by the same author
Francis of Assisi

© Edizioni Porziuncola
   Via Protomartiri Francescani, 2
   06088 S. Maria degli Angeli (PG)
   Tel. +39 75.80.51.598
   E-mail: edizioni@assisiofm.org

ISBN 88-270-0483-1

Cover page: Giotto, St. Francis impart the peace
   greeting in Arezzo (Assisi, Basilica superiore)

INTRODUCTION

In his *Testament* St. Francis of Assisi connects the message of peace to revelation. This idea had grown in him from the beginning of his conversion. The idea of peace tied to revelation is interesting and motivates us to know more about it through research. I was prompted to write this book by the conviction that Francis of Assisi, when he points out to his brothers the theme of peace, intends to say more than what is generally believed.

He spoke of peace in his *Testament* of 1226 with simple and brief words, as was his custom, speaking of it better and more thoroughly than he had before in his other writings.

The first generation friars were acquainted with what Francis meant by peace and how it should be achieved, having lived with him. But the others, those far away and those that would have come later in time, needed a particular mention of it in order to deepen their awareness of this issue.

I have a fascinating hypothesis about peace that seeks to follow the path of those who have done research before me. It is based on the work of contemporary scholars who encourage me to speak and write on the issue.

In explaining the teachings of Francis, not many researchers have focused specifically on the theme of peace and revelation; nor have they examined the many spiritual and social implications of the greeting *May the Lord give you peace*, an important and distinctive gift given to his brothers; a gift which Francis says he received directly from God.

Recently I happened to read the Italian translation of the second testament of Francis inside of a scholarly edition of the

Saint's writings. The translator renders in Italian the verb "revelavit" once with the verb "he showed" and the second time with the verb "he pointed out".

I do not doubt that, as a generic translation it would not be inaccurate. However, it is worth noting that the use of those verbs removes from "*revelavit*" its potential biblical reference (so precious to St. Francis) and spiritual dimension, which certainly was in the intentions of the Saint. This is no small matter.

Still it is worth considering that, in the writings, Francis twice uses the verb "*revelavit*" in the testament of 1226 and only once more in the letter to brother Jacopa: "Know, most beloved one, that the blessed Christ, by his grace, has revealed to me that the end of my life is now close at hand" *(LGc, 2)*.

The context of the letter to brother Jacopa, as well as the two references in the *Testament* is pregnant with spirituality. It refers to the life of the Saint as it is opened to "our Sister Bodily Death" in serene anticipation of the meeting with God.

Therefore, reflecting on the greeting of peace joined to revelation, I realized that the greeting could not be considered as a "good morning" or "good evening". Nor could it be considered a characteristic greeting of the friar, that distinguishes him from the Benedictine monks or Augustinians. To do this there was no need to bother with revelation.

Revelation for the Saint of Assisi was an involvement of God. God doesn't play around to invent words and greetings. Revelation is a serious matter that, somehow, participates in the grandeur of Biblical Revelation. To say "The Lord has revealed to me" is to call upon the Eternal, Who, with His self-manifestation, we believe, wishes to make an impact on our person and His Church.

I am convinced that Francis intends the greeting of peace as a new way of relating with people in order to propitiate a social turning point as well. The wish of peace that is a gift of God, which refers to the original innocence of Earthly Paradise, (as it ought to be understood in a Christian manner) is granted to all people in a decisive, new way, first by Francis and then by his friars minor who, for this reason, renew society and support the church which is threatened by ruin.

I offer the following pages for meditation, with the hope that the Lord God wishes to surprise other people as he surprised me when he led me to understand, at last, the role of a Franciscan working for peace in the world.

THE PROPOSALS OF GOD

That evening in the spring of 1205 Francis had been generous with his friends by paying the expenses of the feast. Nothing risqué, it is obvious, but only a little time spent singing, dining and speaking of love as it was customary among the youth of the well-to-do families of Assisi.

For this reason, or because he was seen as particularly popular, his friends had elected Francis king with the investiture of a baton transformed into a regal scepter.

When they were sated with wine and with merriment, the young men descended as a group onto the street to wear off that little drunkenness that they had taken upon themselves. Songs and a few jokes were shared in that cool and fragrant spring evening. From the walls of the gardens of Assisi hung down the branches of trees in bloom.

Francis was the leader of the company. Then, little by little the other young men ran ahead of him, leaving him last in the group, absorbed in strange reflections. In that joy-filled evening something was happening to the son of Pietro of Bernardone.

The friends at first didn't intervene, as is a good custom among the youth when one of their own is living a delicate moment. But when the joy diminished and the absence of Francis was felt, the curious friends stopped.

"Francis," they asked, "what are you thinking about, that you have not followed us? Perhaps you were thinking of marrying?" They tried to discover the beautiful candidate who would become the daughter-in-law of one of the richest merchants of Assisi. Francis, like somebody waking from a dream full of light that enlightened his face answered: "It is true. I was dreaming of marrying the most noble, richest and most beautiful girl that you have ever seen."

The companions said to one another that Francis was aiming high. The desire of the offspring of the house of Bernardone to become an aristocrat was no secret. A well-arranged marriage would facilitate his climb to the world of nobility.

The authors of the *Legend of the Three Companions* (Tr. Soc. III, 7) from which we took this story, explains to us what was happening to Francis on that spring evening. It is obvious that the Saint, some years later, had spoken of it to his followers. While he was walking "suddenly the Lord visited him, and his heart was full of such sweetness that he could neither move nor speak, perceiving nothing other than that sweetness that estranged him from every feeling, so that (as he would thereafter confide) he could not have moved from that place even if they had cut him to pieces".

Since the authors of the *Legend* were companions and confidants of the Saint, there is reason to believe them when they interpret the bride as the ideal of the religious life. The young Francis was beginning a new experience that we can identify as "religious"; something he had never before experienced, that made him transcend common sensibility. It was the first experience that we could call mystical, but not his last according to his biographers.

For Francis that Spring began a period of uncertainty and discontent. The problem of his own future made him often think and made him uncertain about what he should do. He perceived the presence of a door which opened a world toward which he should go, but with so many possibilities he could not figure out the right one that would be satisfactory for him.

He began to put questions to himself and to look for answers. Merchant? Baron? Knight? Lord of a castle? Priest no. He didn't see that. The feeling for chivalry was inborn in him and the knight always has a lady to whom one's exploits need be dedicated.

The life of chivalry particularly attracted him. It was the time of the crusades, of the troubadour songs, of the memories of the exploits of Roland in Roncisvalle, of the horn with which he called for help from Charles the Emperor, with a slow cry.

So it happened that one night, while he was sleeping in his bed, he seemed to see a figure that called him by name and guided him into a palace of enormous splendor, full of arms and with shining shields suspended on the walls. Curious and trembling, he inquired of his mysterious guide to whom did the palace and all those arms belong. "Everything is for you and your knights," the man answered. It was another sign that came from the depth of the mystery. He thought: Is this not a call to arms and to glory?

The sadness of the search now moved Francis to a sudden happiness. "I know that I will become a great prince", he answered those who asked the reason for his sudden happiness.

He had enough money to provide himself with a horse, armor and a shield-bearer. When everything was ready he left for the south to enlist among the soldiers of Gentile of Manopello who was gathering troops to go to Puglia to fight at the side of Walter of Brienne. It was the first step for the investiture as a knight and the best path for a title of nobility.

The first night came upon him in Spoleto. Being half-asleep, again a mysterious voice asked him where he was going. And to Francis' reply, the voice became severe: "Who can treat you better, the Lord or the servant? He answered: "The Lord." The voice from the depth of sleep said, "Then why do you abandon the Lord for the servant — the Prince for the subordinate?"

Francis replied, "Lord, what do you want me to do?" The Voice said: "Return to your city, to do that which the Lord will reveal to you" *(Anonymous of Perugia*, I, 56).

These manifestations, these mysterious voices, changed Francis. They were clearly perceived as directives which came from on high and seized him in the most disturbing moments of his uncertainty, but which probably had the intensity and the authority of mystery. He returned to his native Assisi.

After the experience in Spoleto the young Assisi man begins a spiritual journey which led him ever more into the world of God; and to solitary prayer. To satisfy the need for intimate prayer, he went down to the little church of San Damiano, a short distance from the gate of Assisi that faced Spoleto.

In San Damiano there was venerated an ancient image of Christ crucified, painted on wood. While he was praying one day, a voice came from the Crucifix which shook the pious young man. "Francis, do you not see that my house is collapsing? Go therefore to restore it!" A totally shaken Francis answered: "I will do it willingly, Lord".

This was yet another mysterious experience that brought him closer to the world of God. He'd been given a task: to restore the church. He understood the church of rocks and cement. He was immediately obedient to that command.

As the walls and roof of San Damiano were rebuilt the apprentice mason came to a deeper meaning of the words spoken to him from the crucifix. He had to grow as the restorer of the Church of Christ. The design of God was revealing itself to him with ever greater clarity.

Francis perceived the strength of God spoken to him in a mysterious manner. It is able to be understood even if the words produce no sound.

A REVELATION FOR THE FRATERNITY

The conversion of Pietro di Bernadone's son sparked the wind of curiosity and murmuring throughout Assisi. The hopes of many damsels went to pieces, as did the dream of Francis' father, Pietro, who wanted to make him an able and kind merchant.

But Pietro di Bernadone was not to be deterred. He tried everything to bring his son back to reason. The townspeople saw Francis as crazy. His father saw the honor of the family deteriorating. When efforts of understanding, love and even force brought no hope, Pietro denounced Francis to the public authority. He succeeded only in dragging his son before the authority of the bishop.

Pietro had resorted to the bishop as the last attempt in the hope of recovering his son. The matter unfolded differently than had been expected. Instead of reconciliation, Francis and his father were divided decisively. Francis even renounced the clothing which he was wearing and returned them to his father in order to place himself more completely in the hands of God. In the home of Pietro di Bernardone the night of discouragement descended. There was no more hope. Francis would never be a merchant.

February 24 is the feast of the apostle Matthias. The young Francis, now living a hermit's life, went to the small old church of the Portiuncola, in the Spoleto valley some miles distant from the city to participate in the Holy Eucharist. He had restored it a short time before working as mason and labourer, as he had already done at San Damiano.

The passage of the Gospel of the day's liturgy was taken from the 10th chapter of Matthew, verses 1-13, where Christ sends the apostles to preach without carrying neither gold nor silver, nor traveling bag, nor two tunics, nor sandals or even a walking stick.

Francis was struck by this passage but wanted to be sure of the correct interpretation. He asks the priest at the end of the Mass to explain it to him.

The priest confirms the intuition which he had and immediately Francis divests himself of the little he still has, and shoe-less, with only a tunic and a cord in place of a belt, begins the new model of life.

A characteristic of the Saint from Assisi regarding a passage from the Gospel is to learn its meaning and immediately to put into practice what he has understood. If, for example, you take any of his writings (perhaps with the exception of the approved Rule), you will notice how the process of his thought begins with Evangelical understanding in order to arrive at an immediate application in his life. Or, inversely, he explains the reason of a certain behavior by making reference to the Gospel. In practice it is as if he said: The Gospel says so-and-so; therefore one does such-and-such.

I believe that it would be interesting, for one who has not yet done it, to spend some time reading the writings of Francis in this framework.

At the Portiuncula, we find another moment of God entering into the life of the young penitent. Francis obediently responds. From now on, in the sensibility of Francis, the word of God becomes an ever more firm point, which restrains him and pushes him, whichever way the Spirit prompts. The young penitent found the right answers for his life. A road was planned ahead of him and he began to travel it.

This life arouses the curiosity of his fellow citizens more than it could appear. There are those who criticized and derided him. But there are also young men and young women who are attracted to Francis' life, though they remain secret about this. The life is too new for one to make a hasty decision.

Among the hidden admirers of Francis is a rich young man. His name is Bernard da Quintavalle. He is a solid fellow and he wants to see clearly into the behavior of this young fellow citizen which so fascinates him. The best thing is to invite him to his house so that he can easily observe him. Bernard owns one of the well-to-do homes of Assisi, a little ways from that of Pietro di Bernadone. We can see it even today on the city street that is named after him, the via Bernardo da Quintavalle. Francis accepts the invitation without any problems, all the more so since he had no house of his own.

Bernard attentively observed Francis' behavior and understood that he found himself before a holy man. He saw Francis, not knowing he was being watched, while he was praying alone in the night.

In light of this, the next morning Bernard proclaimed his intention by saying to Francis, "Brother, I intend to follow you in this life of yours".

With Bernard and with Peter Catanio, who joined immediately afterwards, a trio was formed. Francis knew well how to conduct his hermit life of conversion, now he had a life of living together. The situation had changed.

The matters of the Spirit cannot be invented, they are received from God. Francis, Bernard and Peter sought an answer from God in a way that was fairly common at that time, but not officially sanctioned by the Church. They consulted the Gospel by casually opening its pages.

The *Anonymous of Perugia* recalls in chapter 2, that the three went to a church of the city and upon entering they knelt to pray: "Lord God, Father of glory, we beg you, in your mercy, to reveal to us what we must do."

Having finished the prayer, they said to the priest of the church present there: "Father, show us the Gospel of our Lord Jesus Christ".

The priest having opened the book, since they were not yet well experienced in reading, immediately found this passage: *If you wish to be perfect, go and sell everything that you have and give to the poor, then you will have treasure in heaven.* Turning other pages, they read: *Whoever wishes to come after me, let him deny himself take up his cross and follow me.* And skimming once more: *"Take nothing for your journey, neither walking stick nor saddlebag, neither bread, nor money, nor may you have two tunics".* The passages were, respectively: Matthew 19:21, 16:24 and Luke 9:3. It was a revelation from the Lord: to live according to the form of the holy Gospel.

This was very strong revelation, able to support community life.

So Bernard sold his fortune and Peter the little he had. The remainder they distributed to the poor according to what they had heard from the Lord. By evening, after they had left everything, they had their freedom, but no place to lay their head. A perfect situation for following the Lord: carrying one's own cross without having neither walking stick, nor saddlebag, nor money. They went down to St. Mary of the Portiuncula and conformed themselves to the small space which in the years gone by had been the refuge of the monks of Mt. Subasio.

THE REVELATIONS OF
THE LORD

In the year of the Lord 1226, Francis feels that he is near death and wishes to leave a memory to the friars. He has neither gold nor silver, so he writes a testament which expresses his intentions and his last wishes. We've mentioned this *Testament* above, but now we refer to it with a particular focus.

The Saint begins remembering his early experience of conversion. He arranges it in two points: 1. the meeting with the leper that had changed his entire spiritual world; 2. and the encounter with God through the Eucharist, Holy Scripture and the Ministers of the word: that is, the priests and the theologians of the Church. He recalls briefly the highlights of this new journey, and then he goes on to speak of his own experience as a charismatic man who has involved so many other brothers in the faith.

Francis admits at the beginning of this new life he had been uncertain as to the choice of the model of existence to offer for himself and his new companions. The uncertainty was resolved by a supernatural intervention.

"And after the Lord gave me brothers, no one showed me what I should do, but the Most High himself revealed to me that I should live according to the form of the holy Gospel. And I had this written down simply and in a few words and the Lord Pope confirmed it for me" (2 Testament 14).

In other words he affirms that the original intuition of his new life with the brothers was not dictated by a Canon lawyer or by human authority. It was the fruit of his openness upon hearing the suggestions which he considered as coming from the *Most High* who gifted him with a "revelation".

Remember in the introduction I referred to revelation? It is an experience that we are not able to explain in detail because not every experience can be expressed with words. It must be, at least partly, lived. Revelation is, in fact, an interior message that is felt as originating from the free initiative of God and manifested in His will.

It was revealed to Francis and his new brothers what "they are to do". By living this revelation they gave witness to how beautiful life can be when lived according to the Holy Gospel.

The famous Jacques de Vitry gives evidence of this when he writes from Genoa, in October 1216, to some friends in which he tells of what happened to him in Italy.

After having spoken about the death of Pope Innocent III, about the election of the new Pope Honorius III and his

Episcopal consecration, all of which happened in Perugia, he goes on as follows:

"I found in those regions a matter that has been of great consolation to me: some individuals of both sexes, wealthy and secular who, stripping themselves of every ownership for the sake of Christ, abandoned the world. They are called lesser brothers and lesser sisters and they are held in great esteem by the pope and the cardinals.

"They are not hindered by temporal goods, but instead, with fervent desire and impetuous commitment, daily strive to pull souls away from worldly vanity which are about to shipwreck and to draw them into their ranks. And by divine grace, they have already produced great fruit and many have benefited from this, so that whoever listens to them invites others: come and you will see with your own eyes.

"These people live according to the form of the early Church of which it is written: *the multitude of believers were of one heart and one soul.*

"During the day they enter the cities and towns, employing themselves actively to win others to the Lord; at night they return to the hermitages or some solitary place to attend to contemplation".

Jacques di Vitry, a man of spiritual sensibility, saw this as an example of "revelation" applied to life. It reminded him of the beginnings of Christianity. Francis was certainly conscious of all this and he was glad about the testimony of life — his own and that of his brothers — which he wished to be attached to the form of the holy Gospel. That is the form that had been revealed to him.

For Francis, to speak of revelation meant relating an experience of encounter with God like that of the Crucifix at St. Damiano or of the Gospel at the Portiuncola or of the triple opening of the Gospel in a church in Assisi (St. Nicholas?). In those cases he had felt a particular closeness to God and felt the certainty of obeying a command of the Lord. Just how important was the *revelation* for him, is well demonstrated by his attachment to the intuition that sustained the framework of the Rule offered to his followers.

The *Legend of Perugia* or *The Assisi Compilation* (n. 113; 114) tells of Francis who "resided on a mountain, together with brother Leo of Assisi and Bonizio from Bologna, in order to compose the Rule, since the first text, dictated to him by Christ, had been lost".

"There were in that time a certain number of brother Ministers (that is, superiors) who desired a less strict Rule and therefore they had gone to discuss this with Francis. They had said to brother Elias who was his vicar: "We have heard that this brother Francis is making a new Rule, and we fear that he will make it so hard that it won't be able to be observed successfully. We want you to go to him and report to him that we refuse to subject ourselves to such a Rule. He can write it for himself and not for us".

Those friars who wanted a less strict Rule did not intend to oppose the severity of it, as we imagine, refusing a Rule with many commands and penances. Quite the contrary. By speaking of a Rule that was too hard, they meant too free, such as to leave the responsibility of the decisions to the brothers. It was much easier to obey blindly than to risk one's own conscience. Francis held dear the freedom of the sons of God and therefore he took no delight in imposing penances and prohibitions.

If this weren't true, we would not be able to explain how those same brothers, while Francis was in the Holy Land, held a chapter and filled up the famous *hard Rule* of Francis with penances and prescriptions.

To the opposing brothers the Saint responded in a brusque manner. In the scene given to us by the biographers, even

Christ the Lord intervenes. "The voice of Christ was heard in the air: *Francis, nothing of yours is in the Rule, but every prescription contained in it is mine. And I want it observed to the letter, to the letter! Without comments, without comments!*"

And when, once again, the brothers wanted a different Rule, (this time they wanted it more vague so that it make a good impression when compared to the great Rules of St. Benedict or of St. Augustine) it is reported that Francis burst out saying, "Brothers, my brothers, God has called me to walk the way of simplicity and he has shown it to me. I don't wish therefore for you to name other Rules for me, neither that of St. Augustine, nor that of St. Bernard or of St. Benedict. The Lord has revealed to me that it is his desire that I should be a fool in the world..."

In those days to live according to the form of the holy Gospel in poverty, in love and subject to the holy Church, was really considered sheer lunacy.

There is no need to keep on insisting by underlining the strong conscience which Francis had regarding "revelation". His Rule was the fruit of a *revelation* and as such was to be fully respected. The brothers learned quickly and very well the love for the Rule. They understood totally the importance of a "revelation".

One needs only to glance through the texts of the various Franciscan sources to see the fascination that the short Rule of Francis exercised on his followers. There is a universal veneration for it and a strong attention to its intangibility.

St. Bonaventure speaks of the Rule with an almost daring hagiographic scheme. He considers Francis a new Moses who conceives the word of God on the mountain and writes down the text to be offered to his people (Leg Maj IV, 11).

I have tried to outline briefly some notes which allow one to penetrate the significance of a *revelation* in the context of the testament of St. Francis. I hope to have succeeded. I have done this because I regard it very useful to explain the other "revelation," that of peace. This revelation which has not had the same interpretative fortune of the other.

We will see, in fact, how the *revelation* on peace, through the centuries, has lacked that type of veneration and understanding that the *revelation* on how to live has had: that is, according to the form of the holy Gospel.

This has brought about an interpretative imbalance between the two revelations. The Franciscan theme of *working* for peace has not undergone sufficient development coinciding with the Franciscan theme of *being* according to the form of the holy Gospel.

THE GREETING OF PEACE

Francis wrote in his *Testament* of 1226, "The Lord revealed to me that I should say this greeting: *May the Lord give you peace!*" He acted accordingly.

In this greeting we find the echo of the triple opening of the Gospel in the church of St. Nicholas where it says: "When you enter a house, first say: *Peace be to this house.* If there is anyone that loves peace, he will receive the peace that you have wished, otherwise your wish will remain ineffective" (Luke 10:5-6 which is seen in accordance with Luke 9:3-5).

His first biographer, Thomas of Celano, recalls that "in every sermon, before preaching the word of God to the people, he [St. Francis] wished them peace, saying: *May the Lord give you peace.* This peace he always announced with much devotion to men and women, to all those he met and to those who came to him. In this way he frequently managed, with the Lord's grace, to bring together enemies of peace and of their own salvation, to become themselves sons of peace and to desire eternal salvation" (I Cel. 23)

Chapters 3 and 12 of St. Bonaventure's **Legenda Major** and chapters 25 and 26 of **The Legend of the Three Companions** make reference to the greeting of peace.

The **Legend of Perugia** speaks of it in chapter 67 with an interesting notation . The author writes: "In the beginning of the Order, while Francis was on a journey with one of the first twelve brothers, he greeted those men and women whom he met along the road or saw in the fields, with the words: *May the Lord give you peace!*

The people, who as yet had never heard a religious greeting with that formula, appeared to be surprised. There were even those who responded with annoyance: *What should this new kind of greeting mean?* The brother was upset and said to Francis: *Brother, permit me to use another greeting.* But the Saint observed: *Leave them be, because they do not understand the things of God. Do not be ashamed for their reaction, since I say to you, brother, that even the nobles and princes of this world will have reverence for you and for the other brothers by the favor of this greeting".*

We must be attentive to the story and not trivialize it by supposing that St. Francis and his companion greeted the people along the way with the greeting *May the Lord give you peace*, said in a hasty manner as we of the 21st century are used to doing among us when we say *hi*. If this were the case, we could not understand what we are examining. St. Francis imposes on his brothers a greeting by reason of a revelation, as he himself affirms. It seems odd that he should credit a "revelation" as the source for so simple a greeting. Even stranger is that the greeting should appear to irritate people. It is clear that our sensibility (and perhaps also much sensibility of the past) doesn't appreciate this question. Something escapes us.

To better understand what it is that we don't get, we need to get to the bottom of the theme of "revelation" and then of the quality of the greeting *May the Lord give you peace*. I re-submit then what I have written above.

When we spoke of the first revelation: "*to live according to the form of the Holy Gospel*" in St. Francis **Testament**, we tried to understand what the revelations were for Francis.

We have reflected on the model of life proposed to the first brothers. This introduced us to the cultural and psychological underpinnings needed to understand the second revelation proposed as a greeting to give people.

Today the greeting of the Franciscan, so well known that it's overdone, is that of "Peace and Good". That does not appear in any document, as the greeting of St. Francis.

Instead, it happens that "Peace and Good" was the greeting that a man, whose name we do not know, spread along the streets of Assisi in the early 1200s when Francis was still with his family. The imagery is that of a John the Precursor with regards to Christ, says the "Legend of the Three Companions" in n. 26. The true Franciscan greeting is, rather, "May the Lord give you peace!" This simple expression is very different in character.

St. Francis was a man impassioned with the Gospel. He carried in his heart and mind the greeting that Jesus gave on the day of his resurrection: "*Peace to you!*" "On the evening of that same day, the first day of the week, while the doors of the place where the disciples were staying for fear of the Jews were closed,

Jesus came, stood in their midst and said: *Peace to you!*" (John 20:19).

For Francis, peace was that of Christ. It is a term filled with salvation history and connected to the Jewish *shalom*. It is a greeting perfectly Catholic and rich with meaning. It is a peace that means the sum of every good that the Lord Jesus has given to the world through his redemption. He in fact has once again placed the whole of creation in Eden, which had been lost by sin and has started the journey toward the Kingdom. It is the "*already and not yet*" of the Kingdom. This peace is the work of the Lord. For this reason no human being can say "*peace to you*", but can only pass on the wish "*May the Lord give you peace*".

Francis understood this. He also had the revelation that by introducing oneself into the theme of peace was yet another imitation of Christ. In this way one would help the Kingdom of God make progress.

We know that the Lord Jesus has entered into the human tragedy of hate and enmity to restore that peace that the world had in the beginning, when God created heaven and earth. St. Francis understood immediately that to have peace it is necessary to know how to look inside of the tragedy of sin, of hate and of misunderstanding.

We remember these things when analyzing Francis' greeting of peace. It seems that this greeting had for Francis something new and undiscovered, in its attitude as much as in its words.

I imagine that my readers have already understood that the peace wished by Francis is a far cry from that pacifism very much in fashion which is cried out in city squares. With this I surely do not intend to offend anyone or to disparage the work of such pacifists. I intend only to uncover the full understanding of Christian peace as it had been considered by Francis, and how it ought to be seen by us, believers and non-believers.

Peace, as understood by a Christian, reminds one of the biblical *shalom*; a term that we can express with health, sanity, safety, prosperity, salvation, benevolence, joy, serenity, security, beatitude, solidarity, collaboration and reconciliation. In other words, we can say that peace is the sum total of all goods possessed by our first parents in the garden of Eden and restored to us by the resurrection of Christ. It is, therefore, a positive behavior and capacity by which we can relate ourselves with God, with ourselves, with others, and finally with the whole of creation.

The peace that we so invoke when army tanks kill and destroy, is not only peace brought about through diplomacy or imposition, but peace which comes from a new type of relationship among beings, human and non-human. These are positive relationships and not based on conflict.

To better understand this, I refer to what I call "civilization of peace". This is a civilization we can construct because of Christ's resurrection in place of the actual civilization of conflict. This concept is detailed in my book *Civiltà di Pace*, Edizioni Porziuncola, Assisi.

Francis has a greeting to offer to people and a proposal to his followers. It says: *May the Lord give you peace*. "At the beginning of his sermons, he offered the people this message of peace" affirms the *Legend of the Three Companions* in n. 26.

We see this incarnated in what he did and how he acted. Thomas from Spalato speaks of this in his *Historia Pontificum Salonitanorum et Spalatensium* writing about his experiences as a student in Bologna. He says: "I was, in that year (1222), studying at Bologna and I was able to listen to the sermon that St. Francis held on the plaza in front of the town palace, where almost the whole town had come together, on the feast of the Assumption of the blessed Mother of God. This was the selected theme: 'Angels, men, demons.'

"He spoke with such clarity and propriety of these three rational creatures, that many learned persons who listened to him were full of admiration for that speech by such an illiterate person. He didn't have the style of someone preaching, but of a conversation. In truth, the very substance of his words aimed at extinguishing enmities and constructing the foundations of new pacts of peace.

"He wore a shabby habit; this person was base and his face without beauty. Yet God gave his words such effect that many noble families, among whom the hardened fury of ancient enmities had arrived to the shedding of much blood, were bent towards counsels of peace."

It appears clear that the greeting and the conversations of Francis were so extraordinary that they forced people to make peace — so strong must those words and testimonies have been.

Of this same preaching in Bologna, we have another witness filled with spellbound admiration. It is Federico Visconti, the archbishop of Pisa, who thus narrates in a sermon in 1265: "Really blessed those people that saw the Saint himself, Francis, like we, through the grace of God, have seen him and we have touched him with our hand in the town plaza of Bologna, in the midst of a great deal of people..."

That greeting of peace was the evangelical greeting which had so moved Francis to make him write in chapter III of the later Rule: "In whatever house they enter, let them first say: *May peace be to this house*; and, according to the holy Gospel, they are free to eat of whatever food is set before them".

This greeting of Francis was not a simple wish we give through postcards or Christmas cards. It had a strength that impressed the minds of individuals from every strata of society. Something this impressive able to modify human behavior is not always appreciated by everyone.

NONVIOLENT PEACE

The topic of nonviolence is an integral part of peace. Nonviolence, in fact, is the fundamental attitude of a peaceful person and his manner of behaving. Many think that nonviolence means keeping still and quietly accepting the violence of others; to be so *good* as to not react. This is false.

Nonviolence (which I write as one word to underline its positive aspect instead of it being the opposite of something negative) is, as I've said, attitude and behavior. One expects the peaceful person to be against no one and to behave in a way that does not offend. A characteristic of nonviolence is strength. Only he who is strong can permit himself to be nonviolent. This is a strength of soul, and only then possibly physical strength.

The nonviolent person flees irritation and rash attacks, and knows how to guide his own feelings on the path of understanding and tolerance creating a barrier, when needed, in the face of another's fury.

The wall of restraint is nonviolent. The mountain range that breaks a hurricane is nonviolent. The army which serves as a buffer between two peoples in war, is nonviolent and deserves to be called *peaceful*. I am nonviolent when a child kicks my shins and, instead of kicking him back, I keep him away from my legs. It is the same for an oppressed people who do not resort to bombs; they are nonviolent.

In this way, when we wish peace using the greeting revealed to Francis, we mean a totally nonviolent operation, starting with human beings, but without neglecting any other creature. We don't want any violence or that anyone suffer because of it.

In the embrace which Francis gave the leper, there was a reparatory dimension for all the violence which well-off society had done in marginalizing the poor and sick. The love for the poor old lady to whom he gives the silver bells from the altar cloth at the Portiuncola is certainly a reparatory act for inhuman misery.

In front of a needy beggar he re-composed a fraternal relationship by removing the violence imposed by society. *We are just giving back to our poor brother that which is his*, he said to justify his tenderness. This is an expression that commonly is used to indicate Francis' poverty, but it probably derives from his pacified and nonviolent soul, which wanted to remove any possible occasion of violence. This attitude of his didn't accept social injustice, as we would say today using a more evolved but less loving expression.

It was similar with animals. "Brother hare, why did you let yourself be caught? Come to me" (I Cel. 60). This was a respectful love for non-human creatures.

Francis insisted that non-humans have the same respect for humans, as for example, when he commands the swallows to keep silent.

In the greeting *"May the Lord give you peace"* there is both the renewing of a friendship that had been wounded and the severity that scolds the greedy sparrow for robbing breadcrumbs from his smaller brothers. There is the love for his brothers and the condemnation for "brother fly" who wants to eat bread for which he did not toil.

Violence, especially the kind which leads to war, is outside of Francis' horizon, just as it is outside of the pages of the Gospel. War and conflict simply are not accepted. The writings of the Saint of Assisi have no war-like terminology nor anything of a conflict background. This is all contained in the greeting of peace because this is what Christ brought us; a life of nonviolence. There is sufficient and abundant material to help clarify what exactly a peacemaker must do.

HOW HE EDUCATED
TOWARDS PEACE

The meaning of peace is much larger than the "absence of war." This seems self-evident, but not everyone recognizes it as such. We westerners of this day and age and of this world of wealth, ordinarily see wars only on television without having ever witnessed its cruelty. But in the 13th century, wars were closer and their consequences more tangible.

We condemn war, at times because of conviction, at times because of ideology. Few of us condemn war because we have felt the bite of its consequences.

Whereas at Francis' time there were more vivid personal sufferings and evident interests on each side. The defeat of one side could enrich the adverse side in a visible and tangible way. The juridical pain of banishment for the persecuted was a tragedy, while for the winners it often meant joy and wellbeing. These two sides, winners and losers, could be seen in the same town, among people who you met on the street. So let's well consider the psychological conditions of everyone regarding war and peace and see the difference between our experience of war and that of the 13th century.

The wish of peace given by Francis had the power to soothe hate and thus curb war and revenge. That's fine. It's normal that those who were used to plundering others and wanted to keep on doing it, would not be all that happy about peace.

The friars, and those who followed the example of the penitent of Assisi were able to affect the hearts and behaviors of individuals, families and different political parties. Like Francis, they were able to establish truces of peace. Not everyone liked this.

Francis taught the friars not just a form of greeting, but a way of thinking, speaking and behaving, so that they could become examples of a peace-model of life. The results confirmed their expectations and the different experiences refined the methods they used. In this way an education and a school of peace was begun.

In the earlier rule, Francis taught this: "And all the brothers should beware that they do not slander or engage in disputes; rather, they should strive to keep silence whenever God gives them this grace. Nor should they quarrel among themselves or with others, but they should strive to respond humbly, saying: *I am a useless servant*. And they should not become angry, since everyone who grows angry with his brother shall be liable to judgment; and he who has said to his brother "*fool*" shall be liable to the Council; whoever has said "*idiot*" shall be liable to the fires of hell. And they should love one another, as the Lord says: *This is my commandment: that you love one another as I have loved you.*

And let them express the love that they have for one another by their deeds, as the Apostle says: *Let us not love in word or speech, but in deed and in truth.* And they should slander no one. Let them not murmur nor detract from others, for it is written: *Gossips and detractors are detestable to God.* And let them be modest, by showing meekness toward everyone. Let them not judge or condemn. And as the Lord says, they should not take notice of the little defects of others. Rather they should reflect much more on their own sins in the bitterness of their soul."

A teaching this strong takes your soul and brings you towards a great sharing of life. There's no wonder that the example of the friars had such an impact on people. Imagine these friars, dressed in rags, happy with little food and drink and no human comforts, worrying about peace in families, their hardness of heart, their tears and sadness, rushing to cure them and restore their joy. How could they not obey these brothers who made you see just how much they took to heart the wellbeing of your soul? The concern of Francis and of the brothers for peace was indeed great.

Thomas of Celano narrates in the *Vita Secunda* (and with him St. Bonaventure in the *Legenda Major* as well as the *Legend of Perugia*) that Francis "arrived one day in the town of Arezzo, while it was being struck by a civil war and threatened total ruin. The servant of God was given hospitality in a suburb outside of the town and saw hovering above it many demons exalting, urging the citizens to destroy one another. He called brother Sylvester, a man of God and of great simplicity, and he commanded him: *Go to the gate of the city, and on behalf of Almighty God, command the demons to leave the city immediately.*

"The pious and simple friar hurried to obey, and having prayed God with a hymn of praise, cried out with a loud voice in front of the gate: *On the part of God and by order of our father Francis, be gone from here, all you demons!* Shortly after the city was once again at peace and its citizens respected each other's civil rights with great tranquility."

The command that the demons "leave the city immediately" sounds like a command referred to the evil citizens who act like demons. Should this be the right interpretation, we would have a further example of the need that the friar enter into the situation of strife to be able to offer peace.

The entrance of Francis and of Brother Sylvester in the Arezzo conflict helps us to deepen our understanding of what kind of greeting Francis and his brothers normally gave. As expressed above, it wasn't a greeting made up only of words, but one that materialized in direct intervention, so as to force the quarrelers to realize what they were doing and how the conflict was stupid, short-sighted and unchristian. In other words, when the early friars wished peace, they didn't do it just by words, but entered in the midst of the hate and became active peacemakers.

This example was seen in an Albanian friar by the name of Dionysius. He is in his 90s and continues to work in this mission. He is not afraid to enter the furious hates animated by the so-called *revenge of blood*. He intervenes, speaking of Christ and the Cross, of pain and glory, until forgiveness obtains peace. This has happened many times among the rough mountains of Northern Albania. There I gained the insight and understanding that when St. Francis speaks of peace, he is talking about that peace which makes you an intermediary and a true instrument of reconciliation. There are people who don't like this kind of peace. This is the reason why a brother had asked St. Francis: "Brother, let me use another greeting".

The work of Fr. Dionysius in Albania, a work that I followed with admiration and approval while I was delegate of the Minister General, opened my eyes on many facts of the history of Franciscanism, starting with the behavior of Francis himself. It was Francis who, at the end of his life, gave us a clear example of what this greeting of peace really meant. I refer to the peace between the bishop and the mayor of Assisi.

Shortly before he died, Francis was very worried about the hatred between the bishop of Assisi and the mayor: "It is a great shame for us, servants of God, that the bishop and the mayor hate each other so much, and no one tries to restore peace and harmony." (Leg. Per. 44)

It was then that Francis added to the Canticle that he had composed at San Damiano this verse: "*Praised be You, my Lord, through those who pardon for Your love, and bear infirmity and tribulation. Blessed are those who endure in peace for by You, Most High, they shall be crowned*"

Then he had the mayor, together with his entourage, called to the bishop's palace. Then Francis told his two companions to sing the **Canticle of the Creatures** in front of the bishop and mayor: "I trust in the Lord", Francis said, "that he render their hearts humble and that they'll make peace and return to friendship and affection as before."

When the brothers began singing, "the mayor stood right up and, folding his hands, just as during the reading of the Gospel, full of vivid devotion, overcome with tears, listened attentively." When the Canticle was over, peace had returned. The mayor threw himself at the bishop's feet and the bishop asked the mayor forgiveness. This is another example of how the greeting of peace enters into one's life, making it a pacified existence.

Do you really believe that this peace between the bishop and the mayor was truly appreciated by every inhabitant of Assisi at that time? Once again we have a demonstration that the greeting of Francis, revealed to him by the Lord, is not to be seen as any ordinary "Peace and Good" with which we've filled the world. It's more. For this reason we shouldn't be surprised when we hear that people at the time of Francis didn't want to hear that greeting. It was a greeting that urged the brothers to enter into their dirty dealings, in the midst of their hatred and revenge, bringing fresh air and light and changing minds and hearts. It was a greeting which entered into the life of every single person and the whole of society and changed it.

When you work to change stratified situations and consolidated interests, everyone is not going to be automatically happy about it.

PEACE MAKING

Without doubt, for Francis, peace is the restitution of the human being to the initial situation in Eden. To better explain this thought, permit me to use a comparison and a language a bit out of the ordinary, but may help in understanding.

The Lord Jesus, through the redemption obtained by means of His incarnation, death and resurrection, restored mankind with a spiritual structure able to sustain a life in which evangelical values can be put into practice. Redemption gives us a solid skeleton; bones able to support muscles and flesh and whatever else is needed for human life. In other words, redemption renders us capable of a life in which sin is no longer predominant.

When in the face of hatred somebody tells me that forgiveness is not possible, I answer that it is possible, because we were redeemed and we have the capability of forgiving. When I'm told that conjugal fidelity isn't possible, even here I say that it is, because we've been redeemed. When I'm told that positive collaboration in economic affairs is not possible or concrete, I answer that it is possible, because we're redeemed. When they say that in politics you can only hate one another, I say that politics can produce love, because we're redeemed. Everything depends on our willingness to use that spiritual structure which the Lord renewed in us. The grace of God which helps us is in fact the gift of redemption.

What I'm saying is important in order to realize how redemption allows us to work towards peace. Moreover it's a peace which becomes a possibility of life. All this was Francis' daily bread, in so much as he had a strong sense of the redemption won by Christ. Read his *Admo-*

nitions or his letters to have an ample confirmation of this.

Of course there are those who say that religious arguments, valid for believers, aren't applicable for non-believers.

Here I respond as I did in other writings of mine: I used religious language because it is better able to explain my thought. An interpretation of reality is not done only by means of scientific or poetic, chemical or physical, geographic or astronomical language. Interpretation of reality is also done through religious language.

If I want to get to know a snow-capped mountain in a more complete way, I can look at it with the eyes of a mountain-climber; with an altimeter; with the science of mineralogy; with a botanic knowledge; in its zoological factors; studying its climate; or else with the inspiration of a poet; the canvas of a painter; the sound of a horn which echoes off the crags. It can be viewed in its topographical references, in its relation with livableness; in its tourist dimension, and so on. Each of these sciences will help me know more about the mountain.

In the same fashion we can understand how the religious dimension, which makes me see the mountain in its appearance and its relation with the eternal and its ties with beauty, adds much more knowledge (which in this case we can call wisdom) to what all the rest had told me. The religious vision, which was utmost to Francis, is the comprehension of reality through the instrument of religious language. It is a clear reading of reality and by no means fantasy, which the rationalist shuns.

Such is human reality: we have a spiritual structure, a capacity that opens us towards peace just as it opens us towards forgiveness, fidelity, brotherhood and more. Likewise, peace has a much broader perspective than that which is commonly believed, because mankind was created in a greater perspective than a mere no-war vision.

Peace, which for Francis is not merely absence of war, made him live in a way that we have excellent indications for a methodology. Through his example he points out a good amount of areas where we can apply peace. These areas are paradigmatic for the activity of a Franciscan today. Peace isn't only the condition of a society without war. Peace has a positive side which must be well understood and examined.

The study of how to create a peaceful and pacified society becomes possible and necessary. The Franciscan world has a particular vocation towards this type of culture and science. Faculties in the universities exist also for doing this kind of work. In the perspective of a civilization of peace, there should be workshops that study ways to make peace in those specific areas of one's expertise.

PEACE ON A WIDE RANGE

The relationship of Francis with his brother leper is an example of peace which is not only the end of hatred. In the 13th century, leprosy was a fearful plague from which one fled with terror. The leper not only was forced to keep away from urban areas, but even had to cry out so that the healthy could be made aware of his presence and know of the imminent danger, and avoid running into him. St. Francis made peace with the leper when he met and embraced him.

This fact is remembered in his *Testament* and indicates the start of his new life, "The Lord granted me, Brother Francis, to begin to do penance in this way: While I was in sin, it seemed very bitter to me to see lepers. And the Lord Himself led me among them and I had mercy upon them. And when I left them that which seemed bitter to me was changed into sweetness of soul and body." (Test. 1-3)

In practice the instinctive and subconscious hostility towards lepers, the fruit of a society which sees human relationships as diffident and unfriendly, changes into a new human relationship; a relationship that is friendly and aimed at what is positive. This is called a civilization of peace.

There is a story which illustrates how Francis behaved with lepers, or, more accurately, *brother Christians* as he called those who suffered from leprosy. I take it from the **Little Flowers** which certainly "colors" the facts, but which gives us the atmosphere in which Francis showed his love towards a brother Christian with a very difficult temper. This is but one example of many meetings he had with lepers during his life.

The 25th chapter of the *Little Flowers* tells us of a leper who was staying at a hospital where Francis had sent the friars to assist. This certain leper was very demanding and unhappy about the service which the friars gave him. Francis, who felt himself responsible for the charity of the friars, wished to approach the man making use of his own method.

And thus the Saint "arriving to this man, greeted him thus [note how the greeting of peace enters into daily life]: *May God grant you peace my dear brother.*" At which the leper responded, *"What peace can I possibly have from God, who stole my peace and every good thing, and has made me all dirty and stinking? And St. Francis replied, "My son, have patience, in so much as the infirmities of the body are given to us by God in this world for the health of the soul..."* And the saint went about serving him and obeying every whim of his, even when the sick man asked Francis to wash him. As he washed him an amazing event came about. Wherever Francis laid his hand to wash, the leprosy disappeared. And so it happened that "as the flesh began to heal, so too did the soul". For the leper there was peace.

We could sing here, what we hear in the Canticle of the Creatures: "*Praised be my Lord for those who pardon for love of you, and sustain infirmity and tribulation; blessed be those who sustain them in peace because from you, Most High, they will be crowned*". To wish peace to the sick is to help him to sustain his illness; and even to obtain a cure, if God so likes.

Peace, which is not only absence of war, includes even the possibility of leading to sanctity a thief or a bandit, not only the unhappy leper. Francis says in the sixth chapter of the earlier rule, speaking of the friars and the places where they live: "And whoever comes to them, friend or enemy, thief or bandit, be received with graciousness". This is another way of making peace.

At Montecasale, not far from Borgo San Sepolcro, in a hermitage of the friars, some bandits presented themselves asking for bread. It so happened that, after a few of these requests, the brothers decided to send them away because "they are thieves and do people much evil". Francis, however, didn't agree with this idea when they told him about it, and he organized a way to bring those bandits back to the fraternity, and then back to society. Even in those days this was an innovative methodology.

He said to the friars, "Go and buy good bread and good wine, bring these provisions to the bandits in the woods where they're hiding out and shout to them: *Brother bandits, come to us! We're the friars and we're bringing you good bread and good wine.*

"They'll rush to you right away. You then lay out a cloth on the ground, place on it the bread and wine and serve them with respect and good humor. When they've finished eating, you will propose to them the words of the Lord. You will end the exhortation asking them, for the love of God, one wish, and that is that they promise to no longer beat or mistreat people. If you order them to do something at once, they won't listen to you. But in this way, moved by the respect and affection which you show them, they'll definitely promise this favor.

"The next day return to them and as a reward for the good promise which they made, add eggs and cheese to the bread and wine; bring it all to the bandits and serve them".

There were awesome results. "In the end, through the goodness of God and the courtesy and friendship of the friars, some of those bandits entered the Order, others were converted to penance, promising in the hands of the friars that from then on they would no longer do evil and that they would live through the work of their own hands". (Leg. Per. 91)

I've personally had some experience in this regard. If in life you meet the *thief or bandit* (with these names we mean a whole number of persons who perform activities unacceptable to society), your relationship with them depends on your first impression of them. If they read in your look a negative judgment of them, then you haven't created conditions of peace with them.

If instead they can see on your face a warm expression, then a good relationship will begin between you. If they notice that you're seeing in them those positive qualities which God impressed upon them when He created them, then you can be sure to have made peace in and with them.

Even the human being who may have committed the most serious crimes is and remains a child of God; and therefore the good qualities remain in him, though his straying (guilty or not) may have obscured them.

I mentioned *guilty* to keep anyone from thinking that everyone is a "good guy" which is fashionable today.

If you consider the life of your brother in this way, you'll have been obedient to that which Francis asks the Ministers (that is, Superiors) of the friars. "And by this I wish to know if you love the Lord God and me, His servant and yours — if you have acted in this manner: that is, there should not be any brother in the world who has sinned, however much he may have possibly sinned, who, after he has looked into your eyes, would go away without having received your forgiveness, if he is looking for mercy. And if he were not to seek forgiveness, you should ask him if he wants to be forgiven. And if he should sin thereafter a thousand times before your very eyes, love him more than me so that you may draw him back to the Lord. Always be merciful to brothers such as these. And announce this to the guardians (local superiors), as you can, that on your part you are resolved to act in this way." (Letter to a Minister, 9-12)

Here we see peace and a method of peace as a way of entering into an action of peacemakers.

I'd like to add further information for your consideration. Notice that Francis called the thief *brother*. What does he men by this?

It means that St. Francis had clear ideas on theology and sociology. He's not just a good guy who defends everybody and to whom anything goes. He knows that the person in front of him is his *brother*, and theology tells him this. He also knows this brother is a thief, as society tells him. What is his behavior? Simple. He unites the two realities, careful to know what is true. He loves the brother. He corrects the thief, with delicate attention. Often we are unable to do this because we confuse the theological level with the sociological level. This is why we don't make peace. Peace must respect human dignity.

There is another attitude of life that introduces the greeting of peace into concrete situations.

At the time of Francis, friars minor were popular when compared to a clergy which did not enjoy a good reputation. This could easily have created hatred and jealousy, something which was very bad for the sensitive soul of the penitent of Assisi.

"Francis wanted his sons *to live in peace with everyone* and show themselves small towards everyone, without exception." Speaking of priests, he added: "In this way submit yourselves to the authority so that, in as much as it depends on you, no jealousy may arise. If you'll be sons of peace, you will gain clergy and people to the Lord. This is more acceptable to God than gaining only the people, with the scandal of the clergy." (II Cel. 146)

Confronted with the idea of enjoying popularity at the detriment of others, the man of God knew how to make peace with respect for every person. This attitude could survive because Francis saw himself a redeemed person, that is, a person able to see others positively, avoiding criticism, bad feelings and jealousy. The condition of the peaceful person is to see the positive side even in he who does you wrong.

The legend of the wolf of Gubbio is a lesson for every one of us, even should the story be all or in part a legend. The story is found in the *Little Flowers*, chapter 21. It's length does not allow it to be completely reproduced here. I'll sum it up saying that in Gubbio there was a ferocious wolf. He did much evil towards the population and all were terrorized by him. (Perhaps the wolf in reality was a local bandit.)

St. Francis, ever concerned about his brothers, wanted to personally confront the wolf and was able to tame him and lead him into the city in front of the people who had come together to hear the moral preaching of Francis.

Having exhorted them to do penance and to be converted, he promised that God would free them from the terror of the wolf. "And having finished the sermon, St. Francis said: *Listen my brothers*:

*brother wolf who is here in front of you,
has promised me to make peace with you
and to no longer offend you in any way,
and you must promise to give him every
day that which is necessary; and I offer
myself as a guarantee, that he will observe
firmly this pact of peace.*" The rest of the
story, which is beautiful from a human
and literary standpoint, is well worth
reading.

This way of acting and of treating others reminds us of the value of meekness,
of a charitable approach and of the bread
necessary for life, which also becomes a
fountain of peace.

I would like to just mention the theme
of peace with the animal, plant and min-
eral world – all of creation. This is usu-
ally called *ecology* but I prefer calling it
peace with creation.

We can't speak of peace in a complete
way if we forget the relation with the
whole of non-human creation, be it ani-
mate or inanimate. Talking about ecolo-

gy is very fashionable today and often it's seen as the icing on the cake. Here ecology is not the icing on the cake. Having called it *peace with creation*, ecology rightfully enters into the theme of peace, which for Francis is the uniqueness of interhuman and intercreature relationships. If we want peace, we can't forget that our considerations and relations with all of nature be *peaceful* ones.

If I love nature only because it's disappearing or it's polluted and having a bad influence on my personal and social life, I commit an act of egoism and I can't say that I love nature, but only that I'm interested in nature.

If however I change my relationship with non-human realities, considering them as creatures of God and in some way *brothers and sisters* of mine, just as St. Francis did in his **Canticle of the Creatures**, then my interest for them becomes appreciation and reverence. When I see pollution, I don't denounce it because it's bad for the economy, but because it doesn't respond to the plan of God who created us all.

On earth everyone has his own place or "dominion", if we want to refer to the term used in the Bible (Gen. 2, 15). A dominion recalls the power to "cultivate", that is, to modify the earth in which we live. But this *dominion* and right to *cultivate* must be understood in harmony with the need "*to take care of*", also a biblical term. To take care of means to make sure that the earth does not become distorted by the power of humans. Just think of technological nuclear power, which could destroy life on earth.

So if we consider the *dominion* which the human person exercises, we can't help but to consider another *dominion*, which is that which is due to every other creature.

This might be a new topic, but it's an important one. If man is not the master of the planet, it means that he has to recognize a place for every creature. It is because of respect through which our right to *cultivate* must limit itself from invading the vital space for every other creature. For example, there is space for wild animals; for flowers of the field and for coral reefs in the depth of the sea.

In this sense we can speak of love for all creatures, because this love is based on attention for every creature, respecting it in its part of *dominion* inside of creation.

It seems simple, but it's a complete about-face in the common way of thinking. It's a cultural change. Peace has to do with ecology not because it's the same thing, but because ecology makes peace.

We need only look at the *Canticle of the Creatures to* understand more. Francis wants to say: Don't be afraid of the water that floods fields and produces famine (Francis' sister water wasn't our romantic spring of water, or water which resolves a drought but can also cause flooding), because she is a creature of

God and your sister. He makes peace with her. Again: do not fear fire which can burn all in its path, because he is your brother. Look at his bright side. He makes peace with him. And thus wind and clouds and all kinds of weather; look at them in their full meaning because a storm (all weather) is part of creation and therefore need not be feared.

Make peace with every reality, just as you're called to make peace with every person: "Praised be you my Lord for those who pardon for love of you". And make peace with illness as well, "and sustain infirmity and tribulation". None of these realities are against you; they exist so that you, by means of them, can come closer to God.

The greeting of peace, as I tried to point out, penetrates the entire human existence in its various manifestations. To be able to understand how that happens one needs to think peacefully, with spiritual categories untarnished with any kind of conflict. It will then be clear that the bearer of the greeting of peace can't have a language that is not peaceful. Let me explain.

When we speak, it often happens that we use words which refer to conflict. A description of a game of football uses words such as: to win, defeat, hit, destroy, subdue, kill, annihilate.

Now, to use these terms is not bad in itself. However, they create a picture of the opponent as more of an enemy than a competitor; a rival more than a player; a fan who tries to do better than me. This is testified by those groups of fans who invade the pitch and beat each other up, causing injuries if not death!

I used the example of the football field to underline the fact that the peaceful person needs to be aware of the semantic origin of the words that he uses. If words have such an influential force in one's ability of receiving and making peace, all the more we should be concerned about our culture, that is the common way of thinking and living, because it can influence the behavior of those who could bring peace.

Let me tell you about an attempt made by myself and others to think different than our culture.

Many years ago, in the early 80's, some Franciscans met at the Portiuncola of Assisi to ask a question and to seek an answer. The problem was the interpretation of current events.

We began from the fact that a judgment on current events is given based on the values and the culture of the one who interprets those events. If money is an important value for me, my judgment on the use of money will be preferential. If on the other hand, I see money as the root of every social injustice, then my judgment on its use will be rather negative.

Based on this type of reasoning, we asked ourselves: if we Franciscans read world events with a sensitivity towards the value of poverty, simplicity, a culture of peace, and an openness towards the positive aspects of every being, etc., will the judgments that we express be the same as the current ones or will they be different from those we find currently in magazines, newspapers and books? The alternative interpretation of ours in comparison with theirs could help bring about a change in the culture of peoples.

Maybe it was a naïve idea, but it fit like a glove. Actually it was beautiful and fascinating. So fascinating that it persuaded us to imagine the idea of a magazine which wasn't just Franciscan due to the address of the Convent of the editorial office, but because of its style of judgment and attention.

For example, when talking about a struggle, we would show the diversity and the potential richness of the contenders, alluding to complementary aspects which can be seen in any struggle; and which are avoided in common analysis. For this reason, a struggle where a peaceful person is introduced, can produce means of human growth and of love.

Our dream made us think that this interpretation of human events would have been done by persons who were aware that they were redeemed and therefore motivated by a different kind of wisdom. When it came down to following through with the idea, we became aware of our shortcomings. It is a seed that has been sown.

Intervening in the heart of conflict situations through the force of the greeting of peace is difficult, but exciting. The work of peace is also this: to be in the world with a redeemed mind, with the conviction that positiveness, acceptance and collaboration are things of today and not a utopia of a tomorrow which never arrives.

FOR THIS REASON
IT IS REVELATION

Francis, in his *Testament*, speaks to us of his greeting of peace as a concrete characteristic of his way of life and of how he received it as a *revelation*. Before calling to mind this *revelation*, he had recalled another. "And after the Lord gave me brothers, no one showed me what I should do, but the Most High Himself revealed to me that I should live according to the form of the holy Gospel. And I had this written down simply and in a few words and the Lord Pope confirmed it for me." (Test. 14)

There are two *revelations* in the testament of Francis; not only one, nor three or four or more. One has to admit then that these two revelations were fundamentally important for him. One *revela-*

tion concerns his way of being; that is, what a friar must be in his human and spiritual reality. The other has to do with the friar minor's way of behaving. If "to be" means the richness of the life of a friar minor; "to operate" means the way in which a friar must manifest himself. The way a friar minor manifests himself is actually the method he uses, the translation in concrete operation of that interior wealth which the follower of Francis received as a vocation.

The way a Franciscan manifests himself is included in the greeting: *May the Lord give you peace!* when such a greeting is incarnated in concrete situations of life. The greeting of peace is the Christian way of operating, as interpreted by St. Francis.

Every inter-human and inter-creature relationship of a Franciscan, as well as his relationship with God, has peace as its theme, which means proclamation of redemption and life as a redeemed person. Bit by bit that redemption makes its way through history and peace follows along, peace among men and peace among all creatures.

Therefore a friar minor and every follower of Francis and every single Christian cannot ignore this way of behaving and cannot be content with just talking about peace. Woe to those who stop at words. We remember Francis' admonition directed at preachers: "...let their words be well chosen and chaste, for the instruction and edification of the people, speaking to them of vices and virtues, punishment and glory, in a discourse that is brief because it was in few words that the Lord preached while on earth". (Later Rule IX, 3) To the Lord "saying" and "doing" should be the same thing.

It is good to insist on the fact that the theme of peace should not be considered one topic among many, or, worse a topic to bring up only when there are wars going on.

Once I was told that there were so many things to do that there was no time to occupy ourselves with peace as well. That dear friend hadn't understood that peace was not just a job to be done, but a task and a method of work for every person.

The theme of peace constitutes a central part of life because it has to do with the way that every single creature deals with the whole of creation and with the Creator himself. Placing this argument in a secondary position, will diminish the capacity of understanding life.

CONCLUSION

We have many books which speak of what it means to live as a Franciscan according to the holy Gospel, but unfortunately few on the methodology and working of peace. It might not be clear to us what working for peace means. We need to find a remedy for this. On peace, we have many songs and many nice poems, whereas we have very few testimonials so alive as to build a peaceful civilization.

The same definitions used to understand peace often leads us to think about tranquility of life, serenity in the family and similar things. This is correct, but it is not only this, but more. I believe that St. Francis abundantly contemplated the Gospel of John where it speaks of that greeting which Jesus gave the day of his

Resurrection: *Peace be with you*. He gave us a gift and an order.

I think that St. Francis, when he speaks of peace, shows us a path towards peace and asks his followers not only to use words of peace, but to enter into the conflicts they meet in their activities, working from the inside to make the peace spring up. He does not like spectators in the process of peace, but rather actors, those who work inside the conflict. For this reason we have to re-think our way of working for peace. All is like this, because we know that everyone has in himself the strength that comes from above.

Francis doesn't say *peace be with you*, but he says: *May the Lord give you peace*. This is the *revelation* that he received. It is a wish and a desire. He knows that he's a creature. Peace is something that I can't give. It doesn't belong to me. It's Jesus who gives it, because it's His. Francis knew this.

INDICE

Printed by Studio VD
Città di Castello (PG) - Italy
Tel. +39 758.55.80.85